Discover Ocean Animals

by Katrina Streza

© 2017 by Katrina Streza
ISBN: 978-1-53240-242-5
eISBN: 978-1-53240-243-2
Images licensed from Fotolia.com
All rights reserved.
No portion of this book may be reproduced
without express permission of the publisher.
First Edition
Published in the United States by
Xist Publishing
www.xistpublishing.com
PO Box 61593 Irvine, CA 92602

The ocean is full of many animals.

4

Some animals crawl on the ocean floor. This lobster crawls on the ocean floor.

Some animals stay in one spot and grow. This coral stays in one spot to grow.

7

Some animals can crawl on land. This sea lion can crawl on land.

Some animals can fly above the ocean. This sea gull can fly above the ocean.

Some animals travel far.
This sea turtle travels far.

Some animals do not move very fast. This sea snail does not move very fast.

15

16

Some animals have bright colors. This yellow tang fish has bright colors.

Some animals try to blend in. This sea horse tries to blend in.

19

Some animals have stripes.
This damselfish has stripes.

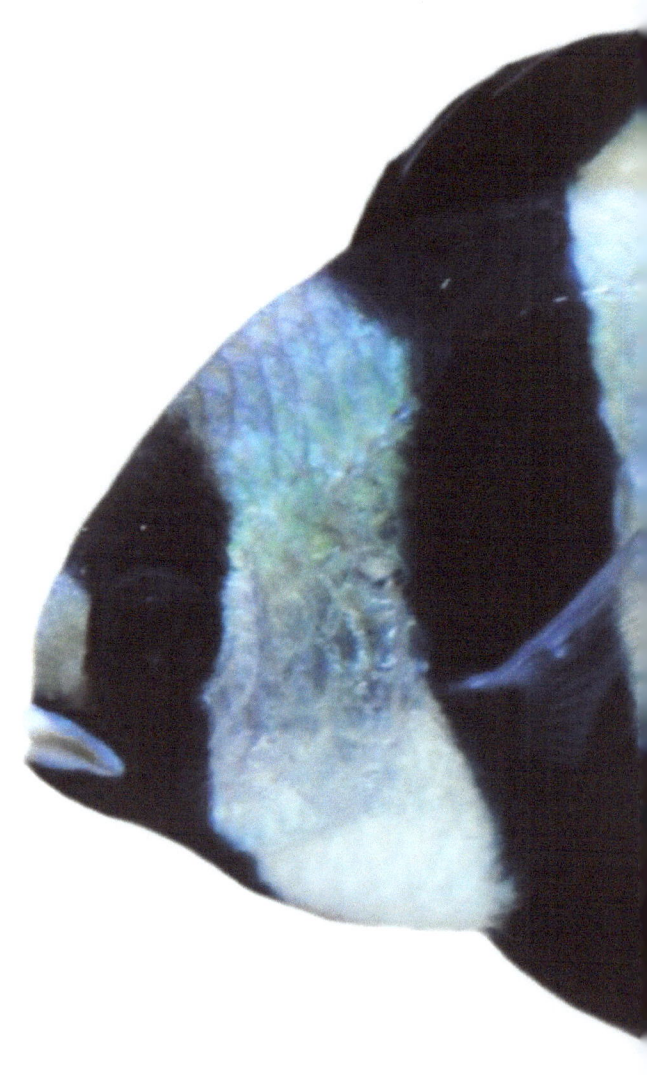

21

Some animals have spikes.
This puffer fish has spikes.

23

Some animals are smooth.
This jellyfish is smooth.

Some animals have arms.
This squid has 8 arms.

27

Some animals have sharp teeth. This killer whale has sharp teeth.

29

Some animals can jump.
This dolphin can jump.

Some animals eat fish.
This Mako Shark eats fish.

33

www.ingramcontent.com/pod-product-compliance
Lightning Source LLC
LaVergne TN
LVHW010021070426
835507LV00001B/26